I0407924

AIR COMMAND AND STAFF COLLEGE

AIR UNIVERSITY

A LOOK DOWN THE SLIPPERY SLOPE:

DOMESTIC OPERATIONS, OUTSOURCING, AND THE EROSION
OF MILITARY CULTURE

by

Bryan D. Watson, Major, U.S. Air Force

A Research Report Submitted to the Faculty

In Partial Fulfillment of the Graduation Requirements

Instructor: Dr. Donald A. MacCuish

Maxwell Air Force Base, Alabama

April 2006

Disclaimer

The views expressed in this academic research paper are those of the author(s) and do not reflect the official policy or position of the US government or the Department of Defense. In accordance with Air Force Instruction 51-303, it is not copyrighted, but is the property of the United States government.

Table of Contents

Preface

This essay takes the form of a fictional speech given by a senior Air Force officer to the Air Command and Staff College's (ACSC) class of 2017. In his presentation, the officer (himself a graduate of the ACSC class of 2006) conveys several warnings and historical perspectives to the 2017 class, including his personal opinions formed after what he considers to be the "turning points" of 9/11 and Operation Iraqi Freedom. The speech in this paper is a work of fiction, and is a mere literary device designed to discuss the potential impact of certain trends within the American military establishment. This paper is certainly not intended to be a predictor of future events. I am grateful to Dr. Donald MacCuish of the ACSC faculty for his guidance and mentorship through this project, and I am especially grateful to my wife, Debra, who gave me tremendous support throughout extended periods of research and writing.

Abstract

This paper discusses two simultaneous trends inside America's military culture – its increasing domestic role and its growing reliance upon defense contractors. First, the appropriate role of a standing military in a democratic society is an issue that has been the focus of significant debate ever since the founding of our republic. The issue becomes even more complex when the military's mission takes on a domestic tone; in other words, domestic military operations can quickly result in diminished public support. Second, recent conflicts have shown a dramatic increase in the extent to which American armed forces rely upon commercial enterprises in order to achieve military objectives. Despite that fact, there exist certain fundamental differences between uniformed military personnel and their commercially-oriented contractor counterparts; these differences are profound and involve basic issues that go to the heart of military service and the nature of the modern profession of arms. This is true despite the fact that a great many individual contractor employees are extremely patriotic, and have a deep appreciation for men and women in uniform. Together, these two independent trend lines may point to a troubling future that includes a dramatic erosion of our military culture. If that is true, America's long-term ability to project combat power may ultimately falter as well.

An Introduction to an Uncertain Future

Good morning, ladies and gentlemen – members of the Air Command and Staff College class of 2017. Today, it is my distinct pleasure to introduce to you a distinguished guest of the College. He has served in a variety of leadership positions throughout his career, including service as a squadron, group and wing commander. He has served on task force staffs in response to domestic crises in 2010 and 2015, and most recently, as the Director, U.S. Air Force Office of Corporate Liaison. He is uniquely qualified to speak to us concerning the future of the United States Air Force, in that he is currently in charge of the Air Force's new Office of Force Reconstitution, Headquarters, U. S. Air Force. Ladies and gentlemen, please welcome our next guest.

Thank you and good morning … please take your seats. I can honestly say that it doesn't seem like 11 years since I was sitting in one of your chairs.

First off, I have to say that when I was a student here in 2006, I didn't dream that I would have the job that I have now … or that such a job would even be necessary. Frequently, folks ask me what I do for a living, and sometimes I even ask myself that question. Mine is a new job, and, according to my title at least, I'm supposed to be figuring out how to "reconstitute" our Air Force. When I first took over this position, I had to figure out what that means, and why in the world our Air Force would need to be "reconstituted."

I'm going to cut to the chase this morning. To be frank, nothing would make me happier than if my job didn't need to exist. As you know, over the last 10 or 12 years, our military has fallen on some hard times. Today, in 2017, Air Force recruiting is at an all-time low, even though financial incentives for enlistees are at an all-time high. People tell me that morale is low within our uniformed ranks, and that Air Force families are extremely disillusioned with our military lifestyle. I'm hearing that some of our folks are occasionally treated poorly by local civilian communities, and that there is declining support among the American people for our armed forces. Essentially, our institution no longer enjoys the prestige it once held in American

1

society. In a larger sense, though, I wonder if these issues aren't really "the problem"… rather, they might be mere symptoms.

Let me begin by saying that I believe, to a large extent, that the American armed forces have become victims of their own successes. With that in mind, I'm going to talk to you about three things: 1) how America's military focus dramatically shifted in the years immediately following military operations in Iraq, 2) how the relationships between commercial enterprises and the American military changed during that same timeframe, and 3) where that has left our military establishment.

As I just mentioned, the Air Force's Office of Force Reconstitution didn't exist when I was a student here; in fact, I don't think that anyone would have dreamed of the need for such an office. Back in 2006, our military establishment was focused on "Transformation" of the Department of Defense[1] with an eye toward winning the Global War on Terror.[2] In that context, ACSC trained future leaders for joint military campaigns,[3] as well as for positions of leadership and command.[4] It probably seems like ancient history to you, but when I was a student here, 9/11 was still fresh in everyone's mind, and we were in the early days of our fights in Afghanistan and Iraq. I remember that many of my instructors and classmates were already veterans of those conflicts, and as a result, they were primarily interested in the issues immediately at hand; that is to say, even though our academic curriculum included military history,[5] students' personal interests also included theories such as "Fourth Generation Warfare"[6] with an aim toward how the United States could win the counterinsurgency operation in Iraq.

---

[1] Donald Rumsfeld, Secretary of Defense, *Quadrennial Defense Review Report*, February 6, 2006, at v – ix, available online at http://www.defenselink.mil/qdr/ (visited 1 Apr 06).
[2] *Id.*
[3]"About ACSC," available online at http://wwwacsc.au.af mil/about/about.htm (visited 1 Apr 06).
[4] *Id.*
[5] *Id.*

That was an interesting time, because – in my opinion – our intense focus on the urgent

issues of the day set the stage for what I've seen during the remainder of my military career.

You see, I believe that 9/11 and Operation Iraqi Freedom were profound turning points in the

history of the American military ... but not for the reasons you might expect.

Not many people were watching this phenomenon (including me), but two trend lines

were emerging within the American military in 2006. Unfortunately, we are still feeling their

effects today. First, despite a heavy focus on Iraqi operations, the American military of 2006

was beginning to see the prospect of significant involvement within the domestic United States,

spurred on by an array of homeland security concerns in the wake of 9/11. I believe that our

federal government began to turn to the regular armed forces to meet domestic needs because we

were "handy, convenient, and superficially at least, effective."[7] At the same time, by 2006, we

had undertaken tremendous efforts to literally "outsource" our own mission – by hiring private

companies to do work that had historically been performed by uniformed members of our armed

forces.

Today, I believe that these trend lines – domestic military operations and the military's

reliance on contractors – have intersected, with serious potential consequences for our society.

Turning Toward Home:
The American Military's Increasing Domestic Role

First of all, I don't think many Americans took note of the military's growing domestic

role – or, if they did take note, they didn't notice with much concern. For much of our nation's

---

[6] *See. e.g.,* COLONEL THOMAS X. HAMMES, THE SLING AND THE STONE: ON WAR IN THE 21ST CENTURY 2 (2004).
(According to Colonel Hammes, Fourth Generation Warfare "is an evolved form of insurgency." It is "rooted in the
fundamental precept that superior political will, when properly employed, can defeat greater economic and military
power" and "does not attempt to win by defeating the enemy's military forces." Instead, it "directly attacks the
minds of enemy decision makers to destroy the enemy's political will." Fourth-generation wars are protracted
affairs, "measured in decades rather than months or years.")
[7] Richard H. Kohn, *Using the Military at Home: Yesterday, Today, and Tomorrow*, 4 CHI. J. INT'L L. 165, 182-183.

history, the focus of our military has been toward potential enemies located outside our nation's borders; however, with the tragedies of 9/11 came a realization that external enemies can attack us from within. You see, many Americans believed – for all the right reasons – that the safety of the American public was the overriding governmental priority in the post-9/11 world, and who was better able to provide that security than the American military?

As a result, the military's increasing domestic role began quietly and without fanfare. For example, as one commentator has observed, "[despite apparent legal restrictions,] the use of a military surveillance system to help local law enforcement catch the Washington area sniper in the fall of 2002 drew little criticism."[8] This was also the case with using "the National Guard to patrol airports or protect military installations, or supplement the Border Patrol."[9] On a basic level, the Secretary of Defense's authorization of 5,300 military troops to help guard the Olympics in Salt Lake City from potential terrorist attack[10] seemed imminently reasonable, and military actions of "reinforcing civilian agencies … with drug interdiction, or to provide security for … sporting events like the Super Bowl seemed, on the surface, functional and helpful."[11]

But there was a danger there, and a few people did express some concern; for example, one commentator warned, "… regular armed forces need to face outward, against American enemies, rather than inward where a military force can become an institution acting on behalf of

---

[8] *Id.*, at 183. *But see* Elaine M. Grossman, *Former JAG: Military Aid in D.C. Sniper Pursuit May Have Broken Law,* INSIDE THE PENTAGON, Nov. 14, 2002, available online at
http://www fas.org/sgp/news/2002/11/itp111402 html (visited 1 Apr 06) citing Eugene Fidell, a former Coast Guard judge advocate now in private practice. ("…Title 10 of the U.S. Code carefully delineates the circumstances under which the Defense Department can make personnel available to operate equipment, at the request of a federal law enforcement agency. Under Section 374, the defense secretary can aid federal civil authorities with 'aerial reconnaissance' – but only in cases related to immigration, customs, narcotics trafficking or terrorism." Noting that the first three do not relate to sniper case, Fiddel notes that during the sniper case's investigation, U.S. government officials stated that they had no evidence of any terrorism connection. Fiddel also notes Department of Defense Directive 5525.5, *DoD Cooperation with Civilian Law Enforcement Officials,* (January 15, 1986), which prohibits the military from "directly assisting [civilian law enforcement officials] in the "surveillance or pursuit of individuals.")
[9] *Id.*
[10] Grossman, *supra* note 8.
[11] Kohn, *supra* note 7, at 190.

one part of the community against another. That corrodes the morale of the forces, harms recruiting, reduces readiness, undermines the support of the country for the armed forces, and ultimately drives a wedge between the military and society."[12] However, in my opinion, most governmental experts just didn't recognize the possible risk. In the spirit of securing the American homeland at all costs, the American military was deemed to be the right vehicle for ensuring "domestic tranquility."[13]

This reliance upon the military was no secret, and frankly, it seemed to make perfect sense. For example, the National Strategy for Homeland Security – the country's foundational document for internal defense – overtly favored a "thorough review of the laws permitting the military to act within the United States in order to determine whether domestic preparedness and response efforts would benefit from greater involvement of military personnel …"[14] Here's a perfect example: as you may recall, the Federal Emergency Management Agency (FEMA) came under aggressive criticism for its seemingly haphazard response to Hurricane Katrina in 2005,[15] and senior government leaders then began to further plan – with the best of intentions – for military solutions to domestic crises, including natural disasters.[16] Thus, a few weeks after Hurricane Katrina, President Bush watched Hurricane Rita come ashore from U. S. Northern

---

[12] *Id.*

[13] U.S. CONST. PREAMBLE, available online from the National Archives at http://www.archives.gov/national-archives-experience/charters/constitution_transcript.html (visited 1 Apr 06).

[14] President George W. Bush, *National Strategy for Homeland Security*, July 16, 2002, at 48, available online at http://www.whitehouse.gov/homeland/book/index.html (visited 1 Apr 06).

[15] *See, e.g.,* Senate Committee on Homeland Security and Governmental Affairs Press Release, *Senators Collins, Lieberman Hold Katrina Hearing, Acting FEMA Director Testifies* (October 6, 2005), available online at http://www.senate.gov/~gov_affairs/index.cfm?FuseAction=PressReleases.Detail&Affiliation=C&PressRelease_id=1113&Month=10&Year=2005 (visited 1 Apr 06), and *U.S. Senate Homeland Security and Governmental Affairs Committee Hearing on DHS Preparation for and Response to Hurricane Katrina*, CQ TRANSCRIPTIONS (February 15, 2006), available online at http://www.washingtonpost.com/wp-dyn/content/article/2006/02/15/AR2006021501475.html (visited 1 Apr 06).

[16] *See, e.g.,* John A. Tirpak, *Domestic Roles for Troops?*, AIR FORCE MAGAZINE, December 2005, at 10. ("President Bush started the buzz about an expanded domestic role for the military in September, when he lauded the military response to Hurricane Katrina. In his Sept 15 address to the nation from hurricane stricken New Orleans, [President] Bush said, 'A challenge on this scale requires greater federal authority and a broader role for the armed forces.'")

Command's headquarters, and openly suggested that the military should even "determine and mobilize the national assets needed to respond to disaster."[17]

Soon after that, Department of Defense officials began planning for a more "rapid, robust role for active duty forces in responding to catastrophic disasters or terrorist attacks."[18] In fact, the Assistant Secretary of Defense for Homeland Defense at the time observed that "it is almost inevitable that the Department of Defense will play a very substantial role in providing resources, equipment, command and control, and other capabilities in response to a catastrophic event … [since] only the Pentagon can marshal such resources and deploy them quickly during a time in which thousands of American lives may be at risk."[19] Interestingly, the American military's focus on domestic operations proceeded despite objections from some state officials; the Texas governor "oppose[d] the federalization of emergency response efforts to natural disasters and other catastrophic events,"[20] and Arizona's governor warned that "moving disaster planning and response to Washington would be a disaster."[21]

That same year, world health officials began to predict a possible catastrophe in the form of an influenza epidemic,[22] and consequent desires for American military involvement in domestic operations became even more common.[23] Again, these efforts met with little public opposition, likely because of the current political climate and sentiments such as the public

---

[17] Tom Philpott, *Posse Comitatus*, AIR FORCE MAGAZINE, November 2005, at 29.

[18] Ann Scott Tyson, *Pentagon Plans to Beef-up Domestic Rapid-Response Forces*, WASHINGTON POST, Oct. 13, 2005, at 4.

[19] *Id.*

[20] *Governors Oppose Expanding Military's Role in Disasters*, NATIONAL JOURNAL'S CONGRESSDAILYAM, Oct. 20, 2005.

[21] *Id.*

[22] *See, e.g., Q&A: Bird Flu*, courtesy of BBC NEWS, available online at http://news.bbc.co.uk/1/hi/health/3422839.stm (visited 1 Apr 06), ("Once the [bird flu] virus gained the ability to pass easily between humans the results could be catastrophic. Worldwide, experts predict anything between two million and 50 million deaths.")

[23] Tirpak, *supra* note 16, at 10-11 ("In October [2005, President] Bush suggested the military might take a leading role in responding to a flu pandemic. The military, he said, with the ability to 'plan and move' might be the best solution to effecting the quarantines.")

acknowledgment by the Centers for Disease Control that "the United States was vulnerable to chemical and bioterrorism."[24] The military's possible role in response to a health crisis was actually formalized in the "National Strategy for Pandemic Influenza,"[25] in November of 2005, where the federal government pledged to "develop mechanisms to activate" those "infrastructure-sustainment activities that the U.S. military and other government entities may be able to support during" such a pandemic.[26]

This is what I mean when I say that the American military became a victim of its own success. Essentially, because of the armed forces' proven ability to plan and execute in the face of a crisis, they seemed to become the 'proud owners' of additional domestic missions, whenever a new crisis arose. At the time, the logic was straightforward – simply put, our nation had a need, and the military was best suited to meet that need. Back when I was student here, I remember learning a bit about our military's evolving domestic mission; we spent a lot of time on graphs and organizational charts, but not much time on the unique cultural problems inherent in domestic military operations. I'm sure that has since changed.

At about that same time, our military leaders began to seriously study the implications of what is popularly known as the "Posse Comitatus Act."[27] Now, as I've come to understand it, "posse comitatus" is a term that is frequently misunderstood. Literally, it is Latin for "the power

[24] Edward P. Richards, *et al.*, *Bioterrorism and the Use of Fear in Public Health*, THE URBAN LAWYER, Summer 2002, at 689, citing Centers for Disease Control and Prevention, *Biological and Chemical Terrorism: Strategic Plan for Preparedness and Response*, MORBIDITY & MORTALITY WKLY. REP. (Apr. 21, 2000).

[25] President George W. Bush, *National Strategy for Pandemic Influenza*, November 1, 2005, available online at http://www.whitehouse.gov/homeland/nspi.pdf (visited 1 Apr 06).

[26] *Id.*, at 9.

[27] 18 U.S.C. § 1385, generally prohibiting the use of federal troops for law enforcement. ("Whoever, except in cases and under circumstances expressly authorized by the Constitution or Act of Congress, willfully uses any part of the Army or the Air Force as a posse comitatus or otherwise to execute the laws shall be fined under this title or imprisoned not more than two years, or both.") By its terms, the Act is technically inapplicable to Marine Corps and Navy forces. However, it has been construed to apply to them by virtue of longstanding policy.

or force of the county,"[28] and it refers to the traditional power of a county sheriff to summon a "posse" to assist him in keeping the peace, pursuing and arresting felons, and suppressing riots.[29] Historically, law enforcement entities have not been expected to perform any and all law enforcement-related duties which might become necessary; for example, in the United States, most jurisdictions permit a police officer to seek assistance for the arrest or recapture of an escaped prisoner.[30] The notable exception is the Posse Comitatus Act, which forbids the use of federal troops for such a purpose, reflecting a traditional American skepticism regarding the use of a standing army to keep the civil peace.[31]

The principle underlying the Posse Comitatus Act has a very interesting history in the United States, and – *hear me here* – we would do well to internalize that history and remember it, lest we repeat it. Here's a quick history refresher: Although you might not realize it today, despite national security threats from several powerful European nations, our Founding Fathers consciously decided to limit the domestic powers of the American military.[32] The dangers inherent in even having a military were a hotly-debated topic at the Constitutional Convention, as delegates "debated whether there should be a standing army at all, or if defense of the nation should rely entirely on the state militias."[33] Even though the Constitution ultimately provided for Congress' ability to raise a standing army,[34] its only expressly stated domestic role was to

---

[28] BLACK'S LAW DICTIONARY, 1162, (6th ed. 1990) ("The entire population of a county above the age of fifteen, which a sheriff may summon to his assistance in certain cases, as to aid him in keeping the peace, in pursuing and arresting felons, etc. *Williams v. State*, 253 Ark. 973, 490 S.W.2d 117, 121.")

[29] Sean J. Kealy, *Reexamining the Posse Comitatus Act: Toward a Right to Civil Law Enforcement*, 21 YALE L. & POL'Y REV. 383, 389 (2003).

[30] *Id.*, citing *Scott v. Vandiver*, 476 F.2d 238 (4th Cir. 1973).

[31] *Id.*

[32] *Id.*, citing David E. Engdahl, *Soldiers, Riots and Revolution: The Law and History of Military Troops in Civil Disorders*, 57 IOWA L. REV. 1 (1971).

[33] Id., citing *The Records of the Federal Convention of 1787*, at 209 (Max Farrand ed., 1937).

[34] U.S. CONST. art. I, § 8, cl. 12.

"suppress insurrections."[35] I want to drive this point home to you – the issue of a standing

military force was a point of serious contention; Convention delegate Luther Martin of Maryland

declared as much to his state legislature, stating that "when a government wishes to deprive its

citizens of freedom, and reduce them to slavery it generally makes use of a standing army."[36]

Similarly, Alexander Hamilton used the Federalist Papers to argue that standing armies not only

push a people toward monarchy, but "place the population under military subordination."[37]

Listen to this quote from Hamilton: "[A strong military leads to] frequent infringements on their

rights ... and by degrees the people are brought to consider the soldiery not only as their

protectors but as their superiors."[38]

On another occasion, James Madison used the Federalist Papers to observe that "the

liberties of Rome proved the final victim to her military triumphs" and that "[a] standing force,

therefore, is a dangerous, at the same time that it may be a necessary, provision. On the smallest

scale it has its inconveniences. On an extensive scale its consequences may be fatal. On any

scale it is an object of laudable circumspection and precaution."[39] For most of its life, the Posse

Comitatus Act has been grounded in these types of concerns, proving to be a fairly effective tool

to limit military incursions into domestic law enforcement. Ultimately, after the passage of the

act, "it was understood that federal troops were not available to supplement civilian law

enforcement officials."[40]

---

[35] U.S. CONST. art I, § 8, cl. 15. This clause was invoked on only a limited number of occasions, including Shay's Rebellion (178601787), the Whiskey Rebellion (1794), the Dorr Rebellion (1842), and the Civil War (1861-1865). Kealy, *supra* note 29, at 391.

[36] Kealy, *supra* note 29, at 391.

[37] *Id.*

[38] THE FEDERALIST No. 8, available online from the Library of Congress at http://thomas.loc.gov/home/histdox/fed_08 html (visited 1 Apr 06).

[39] THE FEDERALIST No. 41, available online from the Library of Congress at http://thomas.loc.gov/home/histdox/fed_41 html (visited 1 Apr 06).

[40] Jack H. McCall, *Mission Im-Posse-ble: The Posse Comitatus Act and Use of the Military in Domestic Law Enforcement*, 39 TENN. B.J. 26, 31 (2003).

Gradually, that began to change after 9/11. Was there some kind of sinister conspiracy to have the American military assume more and more domestic responsibilities? No, I think the answer is far simpler. I might be criticized for saying this, but I believe that the phenomenon was simple "mission creep"[41] during a time of increased anxiety about the safety of the American homeland. I'm reminded of the words of the Pentagon's former "transformation" chief, retired Navy Vice Admiral Arthur Cebrowski. He observed that the "post-9/11 reality" was "that we need a new way to rebalance our overseas interests and our concern for homeland security."[42] In retrospect, his words predicted an increased domestic role for America's military.

You may well be wondering, "Why is this guy telling me this?" Well, my advice is simple – make sure that you have a firm understanding of the proper functioning of a military in a democratic society. Don't ever forget where you come from, don't forget the fact that you are public servants, and don't take your public support for granted. That said, we should all realize that not everyone who performs 'public functions' is necessarily a 'public servant.'

For Profit and Country:
The Military's Increasing Reliance Upon Contractors

Here's what I mean by that. In the early days of our military careers, my classmates and I witnessed a remarkable change in the actual conduct of military operations, with a substantial increase in reliance upon civilian defense contractors. Here's some background. During 1991's Operation Desert Storm, 9,200 contractors deployed to support military operations in the Middle

---

[41] *See* Julianne Smith and Derek Chollet, *The Return of U.S. Mission Creep*, DEFENSE NEWS (Oct. 10, 2005), available online at http://www.defensenews.com/story.php?F=1164780&C=commentary (visited 1 Apr 06) ("For America's military and political leaders, one of the central lessons of the 1990s was to avoid "mission creep," where U.S. troops face an ill-defined and ever-expanding objective for which they are neither well-prepared nor supported. ... Today, mission creep is back. ... Now it looks like the Pentagon could soon supplement its military, reconstruction and diplomatic portfolios with domestic disaster relief responsibilities.")
[42] Vince Rawley, *Changing of the Guard: Revised Missions, Chain-of-Command Pattern Emerging*, ARMY TIMES, Nov. 25, 2002, at 23.

East.[43] Then, by 1999, some military observers were expressing sentiments like, "Never has there been such a reliance on nonmilitary members to accomplish tasks directly affecting the tactical successes of an engagement."[44] Over the next several years, this trend continued unabated; as our military downsized, privatization of military functions increased,[45] and Operation Iraqi Freedom was certainly no exception.[46] For example, during that conflict, "estimates of the number of government civilian employees and contractor personnel present in Iraq ranged from twenty to thirty thousand, making civilian workers the second largest contingent in-country."[47]

Ultimately, in Iraq, it actually became difficult to tell the difference between what contractors were doing and what uniformed military members were doing. Contractors were "maintain[ing] complex weapon systems such as the F-117 fighter, the B-2 bomber, the M1 tank, and TOW missile system, and operat[ing] the Global Hawk and Predator unmanned aerial vehicles."[48] They were also "conduct[ing] intelligence collection and analysis," and "interrogat[ing] prisoners of war and other detainees."[49]

---

[43] Lieutenant Colonel Michael J. Guidry and Colonel Guy J. Wills, *Future UAV Pilots: Are Contractors the Solution?*, AIR FORCE JOURNAL OF LOGISTICS, Vol. XXVIII, Number 4, at 4, 6, citing General Accounting Office (GAO), *DoD Force Mix Issues: Greater Reliance on Civilians in Support Roles Could Provide Significant Benefits*, GAO/NSIAD-95-5 (Oct. 19, 1994).

[44] Lieutenant Colonel Stephen M. Blizzard, *Increasing Reliance on Contractors on the Battlefield*, AIR FORCE JOURNAL OF LOGISTICS, Vol. XXVIII, Number 1, at 4, 5, citing Steven J. Zamparelli, *Competitive Sourcing and Privatization: Contractors on the Battlefield. What Have We Signed Up For?* AIR FORCE JOURNAL OF LOGISTICS, Fall 1999, at 9.

[45] Guidry and Wills, *supra* note 43, at 6 ("From 1989 to 1999, the active-duty force was reduced from 2,174,000 to 1,453,000. Meanwhile the military continued to fill its inventory with sophisticated equipment, increasing the military's dependency on civilian specialists or contractors. 'Highly technical and complex weaponry is flooding the Armed Forces, requiring contractors to be hired to train military operators and maintain and operate the systems.'" (citing Major Lisa Turner and Major Lynn Norton, *Civilians at the Tip of the Spear*, 51 A. F. LAW REV. 8 (2001).)

[46] Michael N. Schmitt, *War, International Law, and Sovereignty: Reevaluating the Rules of the Game in a New Century: Humanitarian Law and Direct Participation in Hostilities by Private Contractors or Civilian Employees*, 5 CHI. J. INT'L L. 511 (2005). ("In no conflict has the civilian footprint supporting military operations been larger than in Iraq.")

[47] *Id.*, at 512.

[48] *Id.*

[49] *Id.*

True, the American military has historically relied upon contractors' services;[50] but, in Iraq and Afghanistan, the reliance was absolutely unprecedented. In Iraq we even employed contractors because we had fielded systems which were so new that the Services could not develop training courses or train uniformed personnel.[51] During the first combat deployment of the RQ-4A Global Hawk unmanned aerial vehicle in support of Operation Enduring Freedom, 56 contractors deployed as part of an 82-member military, civil service, and contractor "team."[52] Subsequently, the use of contractors in this type of role grew further, to the point that contractors were "conducting combat-type operations"[53] that included "operat[ing] the [Global Hawk]"[54] and even "serv[ing] as Global Hawk pilots."[55]

Despite a recognition that using contractors' services in this way could create numerous issues – not the least of which was the fact that UAV contractor pilots could be considered unlawful combatants under the Law of Armed Conflict[56] – the American military's reliance upon contractors continued, with contractors performing more and more combat-like functions. A publication generated right here at Maxwell AFB even addressed this issue in 2004, warning that "The citizen must be a citizen, not a soldier … war law has a short shrift for the noncombatant who violates its principles by taking up arms.[57]

---

[50] *See* Lieutenant Colonel James. E. Manker, Jr., and Colonel Kent D. Williams, *Contractors in Contingency Operations: Panacea or Pain?* AIR FORCE JOURNAL OF LOGISTICS, Vol XXVIII, Number 3, at 14.

[51] Blizzard, *supra* note 44, at 8. ("…contractors recently deployed with the 3d Infantry Division to Iraq to support the high-tech digital command and control systems still under development. Similarly, when the Air Force deployed the Predator unmanned aerial vehicle, contractor support was required because the vehicle was still in development, and Air Force personnel had not been trained to maintain the Predator's data link system.")

[52] Guidry and Wills, *supra* note 43, at 5.

[53] *Id.*

[54] *Id.*

[55] *Id.*

[56] *Id.*, at 9-10. ("…UAV contractor pilots could be considered unlawful combatants [if they take a direct part in hostilities]"). *See also* Schmitt, *supra* note 46, at 519-520 ("[P]ursuant to Article 51.3 of the 1977 Protocol Additional I to the Geneva Conventions, civilians enjoy immunity from attack during international armed conflict unless and for such time as they take a direct part in hostilities. Those who do directly participate may be legally targeted … [,] do not benefit from prisoners of war protections [,] ... [and] may be punished for their actions... .")

[57] Blizzard, *supra* note 44, at 8 citing W. Hayes Parks, *Air War and Law of War*, 32 A. F. L. REV. 118 (1990).

Despite all of this, privatization efforts continued to accelerate, spurred on by deep cuts in military personnel, claims that contractors could perform tasks more efficiently, the increasing complexity and sophistication of weapon systems, and, of course, desires to deploy contractors in order to thwart legislative or host-country mandated troop ceilings.[58] Taking this a step further, some weapon systems were even specifically designed to rely upon contractor support instead of uniformed personnel, again amid claims of "cost-effectiveness."[59] One observer even remarked, "simply stated, it is impossible to deploy without [contractors]."[60]

Additionally, the defense community even started seeing more "Private Security Companies," or "PSCs," in conflicts around the world – including Iraq. Despite official reports that PSCs in Iraq only "provide defensive services,"[61] the extent of these contractor's activities became quite substantial, and, frankly, practically "indistinguishable from military operations."[62] For example, in April of 2003, employees of Blackwater USA battled with insurgents who were attacking personnel assigned to the U.S.-led Coalition Provisional Authority in Najaf; thousands of rounds of ammunition and hundreds of 40mm grenades were fired, and Blackwater even used its own helicopters to supply employees during the fighting.[63] Later, in 2006, Blackwater's senior leadership even offered its services as an army-for-hire in the world's "trouble spots," stating that the company "stands ready to help keep or restore the peace anywhere it is needed."[64]

---

[58] *Id.*, at 6.

[59] *Id.*, at 8 ("...a new Marine Corps truck was designed to be at least partially contractor supported because the limited number of assets made contractor support more cost effective. Similarly, the Army's Guardrail surveillance aircraft is entirely supported by contractors because it was not cost-effective to develop an organic maintenance capability.").

[60] Manker and Williams, *supra* note 50, at 19.

[61] Schmitt, *supra* note 46, at 514, citing Letter from Donald H. Rumsfeld, Secretary of Defense, to The Honorable Ike Skelton (May 4, 2004),

[62] *Id.*

[63] *Id.*, citing Dana Priest, *Private Guards Repel Attack on U.S. Headquarters*, WASHINGTON POST, Apr 6, 2004, at A1.

[64] Bill Sizemore, *Blackwater USA Says It Can Supply Forces For Conflicts*, NORFOLK VIRGINIAN-PILOT, Mar 30, 2006.

What's more, contractors' quasi-military activities weren't limited to entities affiliated

with the Department of Defense. One particularly disturbing example comes to mind: in

February of 2006, "private security workers under contract with the State Department shot and

killed two Iraqi civilians,"[65] even though Iraqi officials and U.S. commanders had previously

condemned "indiscriminate and unpunished shootings of Iraqi civilians by some of the estimated

25,000 private security contractors" in Iraq.[66] We would have done well to carefully note the

anger expressed by the brother of one of the casualties in response to the incident: "I swear to

God that I will take revenge for my brother … they did not even stop to take him to the hospital

… this is their new democracy, this is the freedom they brought."[67] On a more troubling note, in

expressing their sentiment, the victims' angry relatives "did not appear to distinguish between

U.S. troops and the contractors, who many Iraqis say resemble foreign soldiers."[68] I'll come

back to that idea in a few minutes.

Whenever I tell stories like this, many people ask themselves, "How did we get to this

point? Isn't the government supposed to be doing the fighting?" Well, I've asked myself that

same question and I've done a little research. It all started innocently enough, back in the 1950s,

when the federal government "required its agencies to procure all commercial goods and services

from the private sector, except when 'not in the public interest.'"[69] Years later, in 1998,

Congress enacted the "FAIR Act" which required federal agencies to outsource government

positions that were not "inherently governmental."[70] Of course, the FAIR Act applied to

---

[65] Jonathan Finer, *State Department Contractors Kill Two Civilians in N. Iraq*, WASHINGTON POST, Feb 9, 2006, at A18.
[66] *Id.*
[67] *Id.*
[68] *Id.*
[69] Rebecca Rafferty Vernon, *Battlefield Contractors: Facing the Tough Issues*, 33 PUB. CONT. L. J. 369, 376 (2004) citing William A. Roberts III, *et al.*, *A-76 Cost Comparisons: Overcoming the "Undue Built-In Bias Favoring In-House Performance of Services,"* 30 PUB. CONT. L. J. 585, 588 (2001).
[70] 31 U.S.C. § 501 (known as the "Federal Activities Inventory Reform Act")

positions held by military personnel,[71] and the Department of Defense complied, mandating that "functions and duties that are inherently governmental are barred from private sector performance."[72]

Eventually, reliance upon contractors simply became fiscally expedient. As defense budgets struggled under the weight of increased missions and exhortations to trim military manpower, commanders began to use contractors to fill functions vacated by uniformed personnel.[73] Quite notably, our civilian ranks weren't immune, either. Between 2000 and 2006, the military permitted the private sector to compete against federal civilian workers for over 18,000 positions, with contractors beating civilians about 60 percent of the time – winning 11,372 jobs.[74]

As more and more military functions were "contracted out," very few people really seemed to mind. Frankly, many in the military were thankful for the additional manpower they received[75] when the military looked to contractors to fill voids left by personnel cuts.[76] Many members of the public appreciated the budgetary savings promised by a smaller military, and as federal dollars were redirected to private contractors, those companies noticed remarkable revenues.[77] In sum, most folks seemed happy – for a while.

But, bottom line, some of us were "asleep at the switch." Honestly, I don't think we understood where all of this was taking us. Back then, I was a junior field grade officer like you,

---

[71] Vernon, *supra* note 69, citing 64 Fed. Reg. at 33,934.

[72] Department of Defense Instruction 3020.41, *Contractor Personnel Authorized to Accompany the U.S. Armed Forces* (October 3, 2005), paragraph 6.1.5., citing the FAIR Act, Office of Management and Budget Circular A-76, the Federal Acquisition Regulation, and the Manpower Mix Criteria (Under Secretary of Defense (Personnel and Readiness) Memorandum, "Use of the Manpower Mix Criteria," dated December 15, 2003).

[73] Blizzard, *supra* note 44, at 7 ("Contractors have been used to fill the void created by the drawdown in troop strength.")

[74] George Cahlink, *Sharp Focus on Air Force Civilians*, AIR FORCE MAGAZINE, February 2006, at 87.

[75] P. W. Singer, *Outsourcing War*, FOREIGN AFFAIRS, March/April 2005, at 119, 128.

[76] Blizzard, *supra* note 44, at 7.

[77] An updated listing of contracts pertaining to Iraq and Afghanistan is available online through The Center for Public Integrity at http://www.publicintegrity.org (visited 1 Apr 06).

and I was focused almost exclusively – like my peers – on my next assignment and how to just "get the job done" for my boss. If I needed to get a task accomplished and I didn't have a military member available to do the job, my first thought was "why don't we just find a contractor to do it?"

You see, I freely admit that when I was in your shoes, I failed to fully grasp basic principles that underpinned my military service; in a general sense, I remembered my high school civics lessons, but I didn't really *internalize* them. My colleagues and I thought that phrases like "the common defense,"[78] the relationship between "Military" and "Civil" power,[79] and "government of the people, by the people, for the people"[80] were just platitudes thrown around by high-minded academic-types and political candidates. We were wrong. The ability to apply military force is an obligation of profound significance for the American people, and I and many of my colleagues didn't fully appreciate that idea in the context of contractors. There's a great quote, and I wish I had heard it back when I was sitting in your seats: "[D]emocratic government is responsible government – which means accountable government – and the essential problem in 'contracting out' is that responsibility and accountability are greatly diminished."[81]

As one military expert observed in 2005, "to put it bluntly, the incentives of a private company do not always align with its clients' interests – or the public good."[82] He was right. After all, "[e]ven when contractors do military jobs, they remain private businesses."[83] Therein

---

[78] U.S. CONST. PREAMBLE, available online from the National Archives at http://www.archives.gov/national-archives-experience/charters/constitution_transcript.html (visited 1 Apr 06).
[79] THE DECLARATION OF INDEPENDENCE, para 14 (U.S. 1776), available online from the National Archives at http://www.archives.gov/national-archives-experience/charters/declaration_transcript html (visited 1 Apr 06).
[80] Abraham Lincoln, GETTYSBURG ADDRESS, para 3 (November 19, 1863), available online from the Library of Congress at http://www.loc.gov/exhibits/gadd/images/Gettysburg-2.jpg (visited 1 Apr 06).
[81] Singer, *supra* note 75, at 126.
[82] *Id.*, at 124.
[83] *Id.*, at 124.

resides even more danger: the lack of control over contractors' actions and, potentially, their qualifications. For example, "U.S. Army investigators of the Abu Ghraib prisoner-abuse scandal found that ... all of the translators and up to half of the interrogators involved were private contractors"[84] while "approximately 35 percent of the contract interrogators lacked formal military training as interrogators."[85] Additionally, remember that private companies under contract with the government retain full control over which contracts they will enter into, and can even refuse to perform jobs that they've agreed to, if the job becomes too perilous or unprofitable.[86] That is to say, contractor employees can just choose to "walk off the job."[87] Granted, if contractors abandon their tasks, there might be some financial penalties involved ... but rarely anything more serious than that. On the other hand, if you – as a military member – engage in such behavior, you could be court-martialed.[88]

Really, the only "control" or "oversight" of contractors and their employees is by virtue of their contract itself. With very limited exceptions, commanders and their staffs cannot supervise contractor employees.[89] Instead, commanders must go through contracting officers in the event that any changes to a contract become necessary,[90] and military officials have absolutely no disciplinary authority over contractor employees.[91] In Iraq, many American contractors were even immune from prosecution under Iraqi law.[92] Similarly, because the

---

[84] *Id.*, at 127.

[85] *Id.*, at 125.

[86] *Id.*, at 124.

[87] *Id.*, at 124.

[88] *See* Manual for Court-Martial, 2005 edition, Article 86, *Absence Without Leave*, available online at http://www.army mil/usapa/epubs/pdf/mcm.pdf (visited 1 Apr 06).

[89] Such exceptions would constitute "personal service contracts" which are generally prohibited. *See* Federal Acquisition Regulation, Subpart 37.1, available online at http://www.acqnet.gov/far/ (visited 1 Apr 06).

[90] *Id.*, at subpart 1.6.

[91] *See, e.g.,* Singer, *supra* note 75 at 124, ("... contractors ... remain private businesses and thus fall outside the military chain of command and justice systems.")

[92] According to data available from Human Rights Watch, available online at http://hrw.org/english/docs/2004/05/05/iraq8547_txt.htm (visited 1 Apr 06). ("Licensed contractors with the U.S. government reportedly sign agreements that provide them with immunity from prosecution under Iraqi law.")

United States was not in a declared war, contractors couldn't be prosecuted under the Uniform

Code of Military Justice (UCMJ).[93]

Eventually, some analysts started asking how to improve this arrangement, particularly

given the danger that third parties would equate contractors' actions with those of the American

government. One possible answer became the implementation of the Military Exterritorial

Jurisdiction Act, or "MEJA,"[94] which would make someone, like a contractor, who is "employed

by or accompanying the Armed Forces outside the United States" criminally liable if they engage

in an act *outside* the United States that would have been a crime if they had done it *inside* the

United States.[95] However, that law would only apply if the crime were punishable with over one

year in prison,[96] and any such prosecution would be in the discretion of a United States

Attorney.[97] This is in stark contrast to the UCMJ, which has worldwide applicability to

American military personnel,[98] and where prosecutorial discretion lies strictly within the purview

---

[93] *See* the United States Supreme Court's decision in Reid v. Covert, 354 U.S. 1 (1957) and Kinsella v. United States ex rel Singleton, 361 U.S. 234 (1960), as well as the United States Court of Military Appeals' decision in U.S. v. Averette, 19 U.S.C.M.A. 363 (1970).

[94] 18 USC § 3261, *et seq.*

[95] *See* Department of Defense Instruction 3020.41, *Contractor Personnel Authorized to Accompany the U.S. Armed Forces* (October 3, 2005), *supra* note 73, at paragraph 6.1.3: ("...contractor personnel fulfilling contracts with the U.S. Armed Forces may be subject to prosecution under Federal law, including but not limited to the Military Extraterritorial Jurisdiction Act (MEJA), 18 U.S.C. § 3261...which extends U.S. Federal criminal jurisdiction to certain DoD contingency contractor personnel, for certain offenses committed outside U.S. territory. ... Pursuant to the War Crimes Act, 18 U.S.C. § 2441, ... Federal criminal jurisdiction also extends to conduct that is determined to constitute a violation of the law of war when committed by a civilian national of the United States. In addition, when there is a formal declaration of war by Congress, DoD contingency contractor personnel may be subject to prosecution under the Uniform Code of Military Justice (UCMJ) ..."

[96] 18 U.S.C. § 3261(a) ("Whoever engages in conduct outside the United States that would constitute an offense punishable by imprisonment for more than 1 year if the conduct had been engaged in within the special maritime and territorial jurisdiction of the United States ...")

[97] Department of Defense Instruction 5525.11, *Criminal Jurisdiction Over Civilians Employed By or Accompanying the Armed Forces Outside the United States, Certain Service Members, and Former Service Members*, (March 3, 2005), paragraph 6.2.3 ("the U.S. Attorney for the District in which there would be venue for a prosecution *may*, if satisfied that probable cause exists to believe that a crime has been committed and that the person identified has committed this crime, file a complaint ... . As an alternative, the U.S. Attorney *may* seek the indictment of the person identified.") (emphasis added).

[98] *See* U.S. v. Solario, 483 U.S. 435 (1987).

of commanders.[99] Bottom line, MEJA didn't really meet the needs of the modern American military.

Despite these issues, military reliance on contractors continued, with the term "inherently governmental" taking on less and less meaning.[100] That is, the number of military tasks that were considered "inherently governmental" (and therefore could not legally be given to a contractor) became fewer and fewer. Because of advancements in technology, the operation of major weapon systems – such as the F-117A stealth fighter, M1-A tank, Patriot missile, and Global Hawk – even became considered "contractor dependent,"[101] but still, few military members objected. As time passed, contractors even guarded our fence lines and handled munitions during wartime. They shoveled the snow, treated our sick and wounded, repaired our buildings, paid our troops, processed military awards and decorations, and even served as air traffic controllers. Whenever anyone objected, asking "isn't that job 'inherently governmental?'" the answer invariably included, "if the Air Force can hire a contractor to remotely pilot a combat aircraft in the skies over Iraq, or if the federal government can hire private employees to battle insurgents, are any functions really 'inherently governmental' anymore?" You see, we had started down a slippery slope, and there was no end in sight.

Along those same lines, as contractors became more and more integrated into the Air Force's operations, they began to actually compete with the Air Force for talent. At a time when

---

[99] *See* Preamble to the Manual for Court-Martial, 2005 edition, *supra* note 88 ("Military law consists of the statutes governing the military establishment and regulations issued thereunder, the constitutional powers of the President and regulations issued thereunder, and *the inherent authority of military commanders.* Military law includes jurisdiction exercised by courts-martial and the jurisdiction exercised by commanders with respect to nonjudicial punishment. The purpose of military law is to promote justice, to assist in maintaining good order and discipline in the armed forces, to promote efficiency and effectiveness in the military establishment, and thereby to strengthen the national security of the United States") (emphasis added).

[100] Inherently governmental functions are not subject to outsourcing, although that concept may be changing. For a discussion of the apparently evolving definition of "inherently governmental," *see* Vernon, *supra* note 69, at 376-377.

[101] Blizzard, *supra* note 44, at 8.

19

a few military members began to resent some contractors' actions, the industry started hurting

the military's ability to retain members with vital skills. Certain private firms offered positions

to military members where they could make "anywhere from two to ten times what they made in

the regular military."[102] In Iraq, former special forces members earned as much as $1,000 a day

as contractors.[103] Additionally, Air Force leadership started receiving reports of keen

competition between the military and private entities; as one senior official stated, "We find

ourselves, in some cases, in a bidding war for some of our most experienced soldiers and

airmen."[104] To be frank, we found ourselves in a surreal situation; we had "contracted out"

certain functions, somehow saying that they weren't "inherently governmental," but

subsequently nonetheless found ourselves still needing military personnel to perform those same

functions! Maybe it's just my simple way of looking at this issue, but the whole scheme just

didn't make sense.

To make matters worse, whenever a particular function was turned over to private

industry, the military frequently stopped training uniformed members to perform that function.

We didn't see it at the time, but that was a tremendous error on our part. You see, many

contractors recruited recent retirees or even military members who had been trained for a specific

job at government expense.[105] Ultimately, when the military dismantled its training "pipeline"

for certain tasks, the companies lost their recruiting pool. Years later, when the contractors'

skilled labor left the workforce for good, both the contractors and the military were without the

---

[102] Singer, *supra* note 75, at 129.

[103] *Id.*, at 129.

[104] Matt Kelley, *Contractors, Military in 'Bidding War,'* USA TODAY, 31 July 2005 (quoting Lt. Gen. Steven Blum, chief of the National Guard Bureau), available online at http://www.usatoday.com/news/world/iraq/2005-07-31-contractors-private_x htm (visited 1 Apr 06).

[105] *See, e.g.*, Walter Pincus, *Increase In Contracting Intelligence Jobs Raises Concerns*, WASHINGTON POST, 20 March 2006, at 3 ("[There is a] growing trend at the Pentagon to contract out intelligence jobs that were formerly done primarily by service personnel and civil service employees. … [I]t should come as no surprise that many younger military and government-trained intelligence personnel, who have top security clearances, are resigning to take jobs in the private sector.")

required personnel to meet the underlying military needs. Some contractors incurred the additional costs of building their own training programs, and eventually passed those costs along to the government. Because there was no other option available, the military ended up paying those additional costs. In the end, much of the purported money-saving rationale for our outsourcing effort became recognized as illusory.

In a larger sense, members of the public gradually expressed less and less enthusiasm for our military establishment and the people who served it. Career military members started to be viewed as a luxury which American society could ill-afford. For example, in 2006, the military services were given permission to "use matching [Thrift Savings Plan] contributions as a perk" to "first-time recruits who agree to serve longer than two years."[106] Even though this started out as a "perk," this 401(k)-type program eventually became the sole substitute for the traditional retirement benefit that used to be available after 20 years of military service. In later years, this program created a quiet disincentive for military members to remain on active duty for a lengthy career, largely because it allowed them to leave the military with their "portable" retirement benefits still intact.

Here's another one for you – when I was a student here, I remember living in base housing, where only military members and their families lived. I just drove back through that area today, and I saw a lot of definitely non-military faces. Back in the late 1990s, the Air Force decided to "privatize" a substantial amount of military family housing,[107] thereby infusing private corporations – and their inevitable quest for financial profit – directly into our tight-knit military housing communities. These business arrangements permitted private companies to

---

[106] Stephen Barr, *In Effort To Recruit, Military To Begin Offering Matching Contributions To TSP Participants,* WASHINGTON POST, Jan. 11, 2006, at B2.
[107] As part of the National Defense Authorization Act for Fiscal Year 1996, Congress enacted the Military Housing Privatization Initiative. *See* 10 U.S.C. § 2871, *et seq.*

own and operate military housing facilities by renting the underlying military real estate from the federal government for 50 years.[108] In soliciting private companies to essentially own/operate our military family housing, we even agreed to allow non-military affiliated civilians to live on our military bases if the housing areas weren't full,[109] thereby guaranteeing the contractors a steady stream of income.

Thus, our military installations gradually became less and less "military." As civilians moved into housing areas, they also brought along many varied lifestyles, including certain social practices that were arguably at odds with traditionally-military ones. For example, signs supporting various political candidates and causes began to spring up in the front yards of base housing units. Some housing residents were less willing to participate in the upkeep of their residences; gone were the days when an airman's chain of command could simply "inspire" him to clean up his quarters. The result was the fact that more and more military families stopped feeling pride in their military association and some started expressing overt dissatisfaction with the military lifestyle. In response, many of our military families flatly refused to live in privatized housing, ultimately leading to even greater numbers of non-military affiliated civilians living on military installations. As you would expect, this didn't exactly help our recruiting and retention efforts. Some of my fondest memories from my early years of military service are associated with the close relationships that my family developed with other military families in

---

[108] See Jim Garamone, *DoD's Privatized Housing Program Hits High Gear*, AMERICAN FORCES INFORMATION SERVICE, Feb. 21, 2006, available online at http://www.defenselink.mil/news/Feb1999/n02161999_9902162.html (visited 1 Apr 06).

[109] In many agreements, in the event that privatized housing's military occupancy rates drop below specified amounts, vacant housing may be leased to civilians with no military affiliation. This may raise substantial issues pertaining to such individuals' status, along with issues concerning commanders' obligations to maintain good order and discipline on the installation. *See* GAO report at *General Accounting Office, Military Housing: Continued Concerns in Implementing the Privatization Initiative*, GAO/NSIAD-00-71 (March 30, 2000), available online at http://www.gao.gov/archive/2000/ns00071.pdf (visited 1 Apr 06).

base housing communities. Sadly, those times are long gone, and I can't help thinking that our military culture has seriously suffered as a result.

Here's another example: thinking about the housing privatization issue reminds me of how the Air Force also made the decision to partially "contract out" the military gate-guard function,[110] in order to make uniformed security forces members available for other missions that we thought were more pressing. Although the effect was gradual, this action also had the effect of diluting our military culture. Ultimately, no one was called "sir" or "ma'am" when they came onto the installation any more. Officers were no longer saluted when they entered the base; they didn't complain because they were fearful of being labeled as "self-important" or "pompous" - but they should have complained. You see, we're told that customs and courtesies are important, particularly in regard to vital military issues like the maintenance of good order and discipline.[111] Eventually, dress and appearance standards became lax among our contracted gate guards, as did their physical fitness levels … and, ultimately, what used to be called "customs and courtesies" from military members was reduced to mere "customer service" from contracted civilians. Perhaps most importantly, back when gate guards wore military uniforms, they presented a proud image to members of the American public passing by our installations - but that changed, too. According to some observers, our gate guards were ultimately viewed as the functional equivalent of commercial security guards in the local community.

The outsourcing of our gate guard function – while barely noticeable in the larger scheme of our national defense – was a tiny microcosm of the larger issue: the rapid erosion of our

---

[110] *See* Gary Emery, *Civilian Guards Tapped to Control Base Gates*, AIR FORCE PRINT NEWS TODAY, 19 May 2004, available online at http://www.af mil/news/story.asp?storyID=123007764 (visited1 Apr 06).

[111] *See* Air Force Pamphlet 36-2231, Volume 2, *United States Air Force Supervisory Examination (USAFSE) Study Guide* (1 July 2005) para 7.1, available online at http://www.e-publishing.af.mil/pubfiles/af/36/afpam36-2241v2/afpam36-2241v2.pdf (visited 1 Apr 06) ("Military customs and courtesies go beyond basic politeness; they play *an extremely important role in building morale, esprit de corps, discipline, and mission effectiveness.* Customs and courtesies ensure proper respect for the military members and build the foundation for self-discipline." (emphasis added).)

military culture. It was happening before our very eyes, and we were powerless to do anything about it.

Our Possible Future

It is against this backdrop that our military entered the post-OIF world. As I mentioned before, it was here that two trend lines were converging: increased military involvement in domestic issues, and the rise of the military's reliance on contractors. When those two trend lines collided, we were in serious trouble.

Remember, our reliance on contractors began long before the bird flu epidemic of 2007,[112] the New York hurricane of 2010,[113] or the New Madrid earthquake of 2015.[114] As you may recall, these events demanded significant domestic military action, augmented by significant numbers of contractors.

Think, if you will, about the 2007 bird flu epidemic, when the United States Northern Command enforced a three-state quarantine – ultimately deploying thousands of active duty troops into major metropolitan areas, along with thousands of federalized National Guard troops. Remember how masses of civilians tried to flee infected areas, and how Air Force aircraft had to threaten to shoot down civilian jetliners after their pilots tried to violate the quarantine. Remember the hundreds of civilian deaths from those months of turmoil, and how many in the news media claimed nearly all of those deaths were somehow the military's fault; people complained that either the military acted too harshly, or the military did not act quickly enough to quell violence. My point? Just think for a minute about how the military's status suffered

---

[112] *See generally* National Strategy for Pandemic Influenza, *supra* note 25.
[113] For details concerning plans regarding the prospect of such a hurricane striking the New York metropolitan area, see the New York City Office of Emergency Management's guide, *Coastal Storms and Hurricanes*, available online at http://www.nyc.gov/html/oem/html/readynewyork/hazard_hurricane.html (visited 1 Apr 06).
[114] For details concerning plans regarding a possible earthquake in the central United States, see the Missouri Department of Natural Resources' guide, *Earthquake Facts About the New Madrid Seismic Zone*, available online at http://www.dnr.mo.gov/geology/geosrv/gdam/techbulletin1 htm (visited 1 Apr 06).

among the American public in the weeks and months that followed. That's the danger inherent in domestic military operations.

Next, think about the New York hurricane of 2010, when we saw a near-repeat of the Bird Flu Riots … but, also remember the huge numbers of contract security guards that were hired *ad hoc* in order to augment federal military forces and local law enforcement. After the crisis, do you recall the allegations of physical abuse that many New Yorkers reported they had suffered at the hands of security guards? How tremendous numbers of folks claimed that discipline had broken down among the contractor-military-law enforcement personnel during the stress of the crisis? How New Yorkers complained – perhaps rightfully – that their "constitutional rights" had been violated?[115] I was in New York after all of that happened, and I was reminded of the lessons that we should have learned from Hurricane Katrina in 2005, when discipline apparently broke down among law enforcement personnel in New Orleans.[116]

Finally, remember the 2015 New Madrid earthquake. By that time, it appeared that law enforcement entities, the military, contractors, and other federal and state agencies had blended into a single organization. Remember how organizational structures overlapped so no one was sure who had certain specific responsibilities, how contractors actually seemed to be supervising law enforcement and military personnel, and how the American public complained of mass chaos. At the time, I noticed that contractors and military members were wearing similar uniforms, and I remember asking myself, "How did we get to this point?"

---

[115] *See* Bissonette v. Haig, 776 F.2d 1384, 1387 (8th Cir., 1985) ("Civilian rule is basic to our system of government …. [M]*ilitary enforcement of the civil law leaves the protection of vital Fourth and Fifth Amendment rights in the hands of persons who are not trained to uphold these rights.* It may also chill the exercise of fundamental rights, such as the rights to speak freely and to vote, and create the *atmosphere of fear* and hostility which exists in territories occupied by enemy forces.") (emphasis added).

[116] *See, e.g.,* Adam Nossiter, *New Orleans Probing Alleged Police Looting*, Washington Post, 30 September 2005, page A10, available online at http://www.washingtonpost.com/wp-dyn/content/article/2005/09/29/AR2005092901975.html (visited 1 Apr 06).

I was in the New Madrid area for several months after the earthquake, and I can tell you, without hesitation, that some Americans were genuinely *afraid* of people in uniform.[117] Granted, they had already been through a traumatic experience, but they were also simply fearful of the very people our government had sent to help – and that is shameful. The Bird Flu Riots were still fresh in everyone's mind, as were the allegations of abuse from New York. In the end, the public couldn't tell the difference between a servicemember and a contractor; you see, each person in the "military-industrial complex"[118] looked alike, reported to the same boss, wore the same clothes … and even carried the same weapons. To me, these underlying sentiments seem frighteningly similar to the situation I mentioned earlier regarding the Iraqis killed by Department of State contractors back in 2006.

As I conclude my remarks, I have to admit that I'm puzzled at how we're going to "reconstitute" our Air Force. I merely hope it's not too late. For instance, I just read in the news this morning that several key defense-related issues are being debated in the press and in Washington, and my personal opinion is that these issues aren't going to resolve the situation.

The Erosion of Military Culture?

I want to give you some "food for thought" concerning those news stories. Our government has "long recognized that the military is, by necessity, a specialized society separate from civilian society."[119] The result has been something of a historical willingness for

---

[117] *See* Bissonette v. Haig, *supra* note 115.

[118] President Dwight Eisenhower warned against over-reaching by a "military-industrial complex" in his Farewell Address to the Nation on 17 January 1961: "In the councils of government, *we must guard against the acquisition of unwarranted influence, whether sought or unsought, by the military-industrial complex.* The potential for the disastrous rise of misplaced power exists and will persist. We must never let the weight of this combination endanger our liberties or democratic processes. We should take nothing for granted. *Only an alert and knowledgeable citizenry can compel the proper meshing of the huge industrial and military machinery of defense with our peaceful methods and goals, so that security and liberty may prosper together.*" (emphasis added). Available online at http://www.yale.edu/lawweb/avalon/presiden/speeches/eisenhower001 htm (visited 1 Apr 06).

[119] Parker v. Levy, 417 U.S. 733, 743 (1974).

governmental officials to defer to military decision-makers' judgments.[120] In other words, because of the unique nature of the military's mission and culture, most governmental agencies – including our courts – have tried to avoid interfering in the military's affairs.

Well, according to some folks in our government, a "specialized separate military society" simply no longer exists. Here's their argument: with the blending of contractors and interagency workers into our domestic military structure, a "separate culture" has ended. After all, why should military members fall into some different category when they're doing the same job as contractors or other civilians? Is there really anything left that makes the military somehow "special"?

Here's an example: You should know that there's a push for MEJA[121] to actually be expanded as a comprehensive replacement for the Uniform Code of Military Justice. As you might recall from my earlier comments, MEJA was a mechanism for addressing criminal activity among civilians in support of combat operations overseas. Now, however, some are arguing that *civilian laws* should be the sole means of addressing criminal activity by all members of the "defense team" – that contractors, military, national guard, and other employees should be treated "equally" under the law. To the uninitiated, this argument might seem compelling. However, if this effort succeeds, commanders will no longer be involved in the most serious disciplinary issues affecting their troops. As future Air Force leaders, you need to seriously consider how that's going to impact your ability to do your job.

---

[120] *See, e.g.,* Goldman v. Weinberger, 475 U.S. 503, 507 (1986) ("… courts must give great deference to the professional judgment of military authorities concerning the relative importance of a particular military interest.")
[121] *Supra* note 94.

Here's another one: are you ready for your troops to start filing lawsuits? Until now, the

federal government has largely been insulated from such actions,[122] but there's serious talk that

this protection might be going away. As the law currently stands, military members generally

don't recover from the government via a lawsuit if they're injured while performing their

military duties. Today, there's some serious debate that this principle might be outdated. "So

what?" you ask? If the law changes, military members might be able to successfully sue the

government for its negligence, and there's also serious talk that perhaps military members should

be able to sue *you* – their commanders.[123] The rationale should sound familiar ... again,

proponents are arguing "what's so special about the military? If a civilian can sue his employer

or his boss, why should military members be any different?" Just think – how is the prospect of

a lawsuit going to affect your thought processes when you're giving orders during the stress of

combat?

These are just a couple of examples, but as of this morning, the current trend seems to be

that these initiatives are gaining momentum. Interestingly, some analysts are saying that that one

of the reasons for these initiatives is the fact that there aren't many lawmakers any more with

previous military experience.[124]

---

[122] *See* U.S. v. Feres, 340 U.S. 135 (1950) (After the passage of the Federal Tort Claims Act in 1946, the Supreme Court decided *U.S. v. Feres*. In that case, the executrix of a military member brought suit against the United States after the member's death in a fire while he was sleeping in military barracks. The suit alleged negligence – specifically that the member had been quartered in barracks known to be unsafe and that there was a failure by United States officials to maintain a sufficient fire watch. After the case was decided in favor of the United States, principles from it and subsequent cases have become known as the "*Feres* Doctrine" which essentially prevents service members from recovering for injuries suffered while performing their military duties. *See also* Chappell v. Wallace, 462 U.S. 296, 299 (1983), citing U.S. v. Muniz, 374 U.S. 150, 162 (1963), quoting U.S. v. Brown, 348 U.S. 110, 112 (1954) ("[in] the last analysis, *Feres* seems best explained by the 'peculiar and special relationship of the soldier to his superiors, [and] the effects of the maintenance of such suits on discipline.")

[123] In *Feres*, *supra* note 122, at 157, the Supreme Court declared, "We know of no American law which ever has permitted a soldier to recover for negligence, against *either his superior officers* or the Government he is serving." (emphasis added).

[124] *See Veterans in 108th Congress*, courtesy of the House Committee on Veterans' Affairs, available online at http://veterans.house.gov/vetlink/vetsincongress html for a listing of current members of Congress with military backgrounds, along with limited details concerning their service (visited 1 Apr 06).

Why am I talking about legal issues so much? Well, for two reasons: first, the law ultimately protects all of us, so you should be interested in issues like this. Second, you've sworn to uphold the law through your military service. Don't forget – you took an oath to "support and defend the Constitution of the United States"[125]… at least, most of you did; I understand that there are some contractor employees now enrolled in this institution.

As you go back to your seminars today, I ask you to carefully consider a couple of final thoughts. First, think about George Washington's famous admonition that "discipline is the soul of an army …"[126] If that's true – and I think it _is_ true – where does that leave us today, when we rely so heavily on contractors for the defense of our Nation? Second, as you think about the proper role of a military in a democracy, I want you to consider Chief Justice Earl Warren's observation: "The military establishment is, of course, a necessary organ of government; but the reach of its power must be carefully limited lest the delicate balance between freedom and order be upset."[127] Using his words, has our society somehow lost the ability to "limit" the military establishment's reach? Does it matter that the definition of "military establishment" has now radically changed?

Bottom line, we're facing some tough times … but, I'm confident that we'll work through them, and that we'll have a stronger nation and military as a result. This afternoon, I'm headed back to Washington to continue working this problem, and I truly want to know what you think. That said, does anyone have any questions or comments?

---

[125] As mandated by Air Force Instruction 36-2006, _Oath of Office (Military Personnel) and Certificate of Commission_ (November 21, 2002), available online at http://www.e-publishing.af.mil/pubfiles/af/36/afi36-2006/afi36-2006.pdf (visited 1 Apr 06).

[126] MICHAEL C. THOMSETT, WAR AND CONFLICT QUOTATIONS: A WORLDWIDE DICTIONARY OF PRONOUNCEMENTS FROM MILITARY LEADERS, POLITICIANS, PHILOSOPHERS, WRITERS AND OTHERS 36 (1997).

[127] Laird v. Tatum, 408 U.S. 1, 19-20 (1972), citing Chief Justice Earl Warren, _The Bill of Rights and the Military_, 37 N. Y. U. L. REV. 181, 182 (1962).

www.ingramcontent.com/pod-product-compliance
Lightning Source LLC
Chambersburg PA
CBHW081541280526
45788CB00010B/3318

* 9 7 8 1 5 4 3 0 5 2 8 1 7 *